Democracy
in
Silhouette
Poems

Democracy in Silhouette
Poems

T. L. Cooper

Copyright © 2020 T. L. Cooper
All rights reserved. Published in the United States by The TLC Press.

ISBN-13: 978-1-943736-04-1

DEDICATION

For my Daddy, Dean Cooper, and my Grandpa, Glen Stamm, whose political discussions taught me that political differences can enlighten rather than destroy if handled as a tool to find common ground instead of divide people.

Holy Yesterday

We look back
Through memory hazed lenses
Seeing only what made hearts sing
Creating deities in what was
Ignoring all that didn't work
Worshiping a simpler life
That wasn't so simple
Driving home an idea of home
That never existed
Fantasy imprisoning reality
We sing praises of non-existent moments
Bemoaning the lives we lead
Wishing for a past we couldn't wait to escape
Undoing progress in the name of traditional values
Dismissing the impact on real lives
Ignoring why we needed progress then
We stand on the sidelines of our own lives
Lives that aren't as perfect as the fantasies we cultivated
Longing for an existence created by our
Memory hazed lenses of days gone by
Crying over a reality we never lived
Listening to one more fictional sermon
Dictated from on high about the destruction of tradition
Omitting all the atrocities that accompanied those traditions
Bowing down to the deities of memory
Without ever stopping to see
The consequences of erasing progress
So go ahead bow down
Sing your praises to Holy Yesterday…
You'll never find what you're looking for
In memory hazed lenses distorting reality

Me? I think I'll embrace
Tomorrow
And leave the deity of yesterday
Shelved behind the progress of today
Because, honestly, I have no desire to worship
Holy Yesterday

Art of Democracy

A democracy's success
Depends on the people.
Knowledgeable people
Cast the best votes.
Dreams of yesterday
Do not a democracy make.
Change comes with
The change in society
A democracy must keep pace
Or it falls prey to dissolution
By a thousand and one little slices
To the rights of the people
To elect representatives
Who bring their concerns
To the table in knowledgeable ways.
A democracy in ruins begins
When the agreed upon rules
Are flouted by the representatives
Who have stopped listening to
The people they represent.
The art of democracy
Comes with the participation
Of the people who openly communicate
With their representatives
And vote their values
The question is
Can democracy be saved
Once it's been perverted
For the good of the few
Destroying the rights
Of anyone who gets in the way

Money isn't democracy
Money abuses democracy
And leaves the people
Flailing to find their footing.
So I ask you
Do you care about
The art of democracy?

Oh, Democracy, What Say You

We wax poetic
Spouting democracy
As our excuse for
Superior attitudes
Arrogance bleeds
From the word
As we say it with
Religious fervor
Pretending it is
Uncorruptible
Oh, democracy
Of the people
By the people
For the people
Sounds so good
In theory
But is this thing
We call democracy
What we really live?
Is it even what we really want?
Far too often the ideology
Of democracy
Gets in the way of the
Powers that be
Yet they scream
Democracy every time
The people demand
They embrace
Of the people
By the people
For the people

Then again
The willfully ignorant
Tend to destroy
Democracy for everyone
What a beautiful idea
This democracy
Where the people
Truly have a say
Oh, democracy
How you've been tainted
By those who abuse your principles
Oh, democracy, what say you
Oh, democracy

Corpocracy

When a democracy
Becomes a corpocracy
What is one person to do?
Scream about semantics
Such as the difference between
Democracy and democratic republic
Decry socialism
Rail against their neighbor
Blame the person who doesn't look like them
Oh, yes, buy right into the divisiveness
The corpocracy sells everyday
At bargain basement prices
What happens if we…
Refuse to buy their second lots
At bottom prices
Because the cost of the sale is too high
When the divisiveness costs us our
Bargaining power
Thinking we got a break we didn't
While they laugh as they
Stuff their overflowing pockets
Leaving all the rest of us
To hope a few cents spill
Onto our lives
Even as they wrench away
Our hopes and dreams
Of making enough
To not work our fingers to the bone
To line their silk pockets
So they buy the politicians

With promises of untold riches and power
If only the politicians will do the dirty work for them
Keep the masses scrambling to earn a living
While keeping them from uniting
Because united, the masses can break down
The walls they've built to protect themselves
From the reality of the everyday person
Yes, that's what you get when corpocracy
Invades a democracy
The democracy becomes one more weapon
To keep the masses in line
So the corporations can keep increasing
Their wealth and power
So what do you say?
Come, join me in a fight against corpocracy?

In a World Gone Fascist

In a world gone fascist
Where does love fit in
How can acceptance breathe
What does expression mean
When do we feel free
Why exist at all
There's so much at stake
Yet so few see
Those words...
Those promises...
Those vows...
The hatred inflamed
To excite vitriol
Is all acceptable until...
It makes its way to
You
You
You
Because in a world gone fascist
No one is immune from the spread of hate
From the power that oppresses
From the greed that destroys
And for what?
A sense of superiority over others
You had that one moment
When the powers that be
Aligned with you
Until they didn't
And then you realized
The people you gleefully oppressed and suppressed
Were more like you than you knew

Suddenly, it's too late to backtrack
To set right the wrong
To fight for a present
That promises a liberated future
A future at all
As you turn to face
Your accuser
Your abuser
Your oppressor
Restrained, beaten down, cut wide open
What else can you do as you surrender
But remember
The moment when you had the choice
And you chose
And you chose
And you chose
This
This
This
Closing your eyes and sighing
One final tear
Not from physical pain
But of regret
Oh, how you welcome
That one last blow
Feeling it's your just punishment
As finally you exhale
One last breath
Let go
Go dark
Leaving behind
What you chose
When you opted
For a world turned fascist

Without a clue
Because you voted your fear and resentment
Because you didn't really pay attention
Because you dismissed what you didn't want to hear
And now
A world turned fascist
Is what your children inherit
Never knowing the freedom
You once enjoyed
Maybe they will even learn to be happy
In a world turned fascist
Until the day they rise up
Take back freedom
Liberate themselves
Because the things you oppress and suppress
Never really die
They only go underground
Fighting and waiting and watching
Working their way back to the surface
Because you can never regulate out of existence
What lives in the genes
It finds a way to survive
Even when hope seems nonexistent
Still lives in someone's heart and memory
And, someday, even if your children don't rise up
Against a world turned fascist
The Earth will

Politician

Lie teller
Story maker
Bribe taker
Greed lover
Money changer
Truth distorter
Fact manipulator
Law deviator
Progress thief
Corporate philanderer
Persona holder
Country destroyer
Self-important entertainer
Useless shill
Oh, what would we do
Without
Politicians to destroy
Hope for progress
The future for us all

When They Come

The tears slid down her face
Not a word she whispered
Not a word she heard
Her heart chopped into pieces
One-inch pieces perfect for sautéing
But she knew they were too tough
For chewing
No matter how finely chopped
By a world that cast her to the sidelines
Called her a misfit
Because she didn't fit the mold assigned her
She defied expectations and stood a little taller
Her tears falling on the chopped pieces of her heart
Looking up and down the row of people cast out
Just like her
She saw all their hearts chopped and tossed aside
As if they didn't matter
She leaned forward and lifted the pieces of her heart into her hands
Let her tears fall onto the pieces
As she held them tenderly
Magically they began to heal
Her tears the glue to pull them back together
She watched as all the others beside her
Lifted their hearts and let their tears fall on them
As they embraced their scarred hearts together
They faced an uncertain world
That cast them out
In a nation that prided itself on freedom
A freedom she'd never felt
She opened her mouth to speak
And felt her heart thump in her chest

They might have chopped her heart into pieces
But they'd have to kill her to keep it that way
She raised her arm and let out a battle cry
Let them come
Let them come
Let them come
She linked arms with her neighbors
Who linked arms with their neighbors
Until they formed a chain of pieced together hearts
Fighting for the freedom they'd always dreamed possible
They marched forward back into the fray
Refusing to be sidelined anymore
More scarred hearts joined them with each step they took
Arms linked because they all knew what I know
When they come for my sister
When they come for my brother
When they come for my neighbor
When they come for my lover
When they come for my friend
When they come for you
They come for me…

Storm

A branch in the wind
Taking away this need
A whisper through the leaves
Drying on my eaves
A flash of lightning
Illuminating the dark
You left in your wake
A crash of thunder
Rolling into my memories
Every lost moment
Just beyond my reach
Where I could've embraced
The rain on my face
Where injustice and justice
Stormed against each other
In the ether of words
Pounding the ground
Threatening to flood
The world in its twists and turns
As the winds grew faster and stronger
Seeking to destroy the peace
We never quite managed to create
In the world where only the most
Destructive storm receives any notice

Stand with Me

Stand with me
Against the tyranny
We see in the light of day
Even as it tries to hide in the shadows
Calling itself democracy
But dismissing the people's will
For the needs of the greedy
We can bring down the oligarchy
If we refuse to be bought
By the flash and the spectacle
Distracting us from the deception
Designed to keep us divided
So we can't see the commonalities we share
Because if we find a way to unite
We will be the ones with the power
To stand strong against those
Who seek to destroy
Everything we've created
Through the decades
All for the benefit of a few
But, if you and I stand hand in hand
Ignore what they tell us about each other
Really talk and find common ground
We can protect all that we hold dear
Atone for the wrongs of our ancestors
Then, and only then, can we stop to breathe
Because every step forward terrifies those
Who seek to keep us fighting each other
So we can't fight them
To protect each other
So, please my friend,

Stand with me
Because together we can win

The Power of Walls
(written on the 25th anniversary of the fall of the Berlin Wall)

Today…
A wall of balloons floats to the clouds
Twenty-five years ago…
A wall crashed to the ground in the same place
Pieces of that wall now art exhibits around the world
Giving history to division broken down
The power of unity to liberate peace
Not every exchange leads us to truly see each other
We scream about peace
As we hurl insults around the world
No walls available to catch the sound
Reverberate the pain back to our hearts
It travels across the seas and through the air
Pained expressions of hate and misunderstanding
Compassion killed in the fear of uncertainty
Doubt flooding us with anger
Forcing us to consider the walls we could build
To keep out the so called riff-raff
Do we learn nothing from history?
How can we stay silent when peace is at stake?
Dividing human being from human being
Erecting cages for our entertainment
Driving out the voices of dissent
We stand on the side of walls we can't see
Bemoaning the walls others build
Screaming the injustice of those who divide
Never seeing how our own walls create
Just as much discord and disenfranchisement
As balloons lift into the moonlit sky
Leaving behind the light of remembrance

We must see that only through unity
Do we find our humanity
So I ask you
Do you spend your days
Building walls…
Or
Tearing down walls…

Hey World

Hey World
Remember me
I had so many plans for you
You and I were going to change you
Well, I planned to change you
I wanted to make you better
Better for all your inhabitants
So we would all find harmony
And peace would come to roost
People would choose love over hate
People would choose peace over war
People would choose kindness over violence
People would see value in other people
Oh, I had such plans for you
With me at the helm
Speaking for all those who felt
You'd betrayed them
Then one day my world went dark
I hid in first one closet and then another
Trying to not be seen while still
Trying to make you a better place
Thinking you and I were conspiring
On your improvement
While I ignored by own issues with life
My own issues with you
Hiding in my closet
Dressing up in my façade each morning
To face you pretending I knew what I was doing
When really I just wanted to run away from you
Hide deep in that walk-in closet behind
The clothes and the shoes that spoke a confidence

I didn't feel on the inside
But as often happens when I stripped down
In front of the mirror
I couldn't look myself in the eye
Because everything I thought I'd do to
Make you better struggled to be what I wasn't
Visible for all to see
So today when I say "Hey World"
I have a whole new understanding
Of just how hard it is to exact change in you
To do so I must step out of the closet
And stop cowering in the shadows
Afraid you'll attack me with all the vengeance in your core
So, Hey World, if you're up for the challenge
I'm here to be seen and to be heard
We can collaborate if you promise
To keep up your end of our deal
If not, you still aren't going to stop me
From trying to make you
A better place for all your inhabitants

Something to Behold

We celebrate violence
Like it's an achievement
We won this war
We fought this battle
We killed this many people
The number climbing and climbing
We killed more people than they did
As if that's a thing of which to be proud
But, oh, that violence is something to behold

We stood above starving children and offered crumbs
While lecturing them on the perils of the poverty they can't escape
We stood over the rape victims' faces scrunched in disbelief
Telling her to dry her tears, get up, and get on with life
But, oh, that violence is something to behold

We spread violence across our screens, through our books, in our music
Then we wonder why we turn to violence as if it offers a secret solution
Only to be surprised when the dead don't arise and walk off the stage
Only to be dumbfounded when the starving child dies of malnutrition
Only to be irritated when the rape victim doesn't want to be touched
But, oh, that violence is something to behold

Then we turn to the news to hear the day's latest violence
A teenager – a child really – shot up a school
Another teenager shot himself after being bullied
A young man laughed as he beat his girlfriend just like his dad beats his mom
But, oh, that violence is something to behold

A man sends pipe bombs to those he deems political enemies
Another man stockpiles weapons and plans a mass murder

Yet another man shoots up a place of worship
Because the other…
The other must be taken out or at least put in their place
But, oh, that violence is something to behold

We moan and we cry over the loss
We offer thoughts and prayers
We vow never again
But, oh, that violence is something to behold

Then we pour a drink
Turn on the television
Eat death on a bun
Sing along to violence in the song
Numb out the violence with violence
But, oh, that violence is something to behold

Then we wonder why the world around us is so violent
When all we want is peace
But, oh, that violence is something to behold

Left, Center, Right

Left, Center, Right
Which is correct?
What do we find
Taking sides

Progress, continuity, tradition
Can we honor the future while pursuing change?
Can we see the moment without losing the goal?
Can we find a way to hear each other without screaming?
Where do we find
The truth of the matter
Is it really somewhere in the middle?

Unlikely

Sometimes evidence is evidence is evidence
There's nothing to debate
When we understand
Opinions aren't facts
Belief doesn't equal truth
Faith isn't a reason
So I ask time and again

How do we bridge the gulfs expanding between us
When we refuse to even acknowledge they exist?

Lines on the Window

Lines on the window
Obscuring my view
My world between these walls
Contained and safe
Keeping you out
Keeping me in
I see you
You see me
On opposite sides of those lines
We hide from that which unites us
In the safety of what divides us
Unwilling to wipe away the
Lines on the window
Streaks of dirt and water dried on the window
The good and bad we hide inside our individual worlds
To keep the violence alive
While proclaiming we're seeking peace
When will we address the reality
Neither of us is all good or all bad
We are instead humans hiding
Behind the lines of dogma
That keep us isolated
In the prisons of our minds and hearts
Instead of allowing ourselves the liberation
Of embracing all we could be
If we could just see past
The lines on the window

Twisted

I twisted
This way and that
Contorted myself
To see your point of view
But you stood rigid
Unwilling to bend
No matter how much
Pain your beliefs inflicted
The facts didn't matter
Yet I worried about hurting
Your feelings
While you didn't give a damn
About destroying my life

Not a Reality Show

This is real life
The stakes are too high
For the games we play
Reputations taking hit after hit
With lies spoken far too smoothly
Confident the audience won't care
As long as their beliefs are fed
Hatred and vitriol spewing from smiles
While facts are dismissed with ease
And opinions rule the day
Just so long as the promises feed the fear
That keeps everyone on edge
Knowing that tomorrow denial will flow
Just as easily as the deception it denies
Confessions made and excused
Accusations exalted regardless of validity
All because it's far more entertaining
To watch conflict than to embrace the boring work
The hard work of actually doing the job
Far removed from the rhetoric that brings cheers
Rational thought caught up in a frenzy of emotion
While the music warns of approaching doom
That doesn't really exist
But we must keep everyone on edge
Creating chaos by not cooperating
Then blaming the other for
Exactly what one did
Oh, if the focus remains fuzzy
The deception can grow roots
That will encompass the entire world
To feed a few pockets of greed

To keep the divisions rife with hatred
Because if they should unite
This reality show will go up in flames
Oh, wait, this fire is already burning out of control
While those in power scream only they can control it
To keep the masses silent in their little lives
Feeding the pockets of the few
From the work of the many
Turning citizen against citizen
To protect their power, their privilege, their prestige
All the while feeding the flames of fear
As if at the end of the show
A happy ending awaits all
But, this is not a reality show
It's real life
With real consequences
For real people
In real situations
For real purposes
Needing real answers
Not answers for ratings
Like we're in some damn
Reality show
I urge you
As much as you enjoy the entertainment
To think of the reality of life
In a complex world
With complex problems
Intertwined with complex relationships
The answers aren't so simple
As what makes you feel entertained
Please stop treating the future
Like some damned reality show
Because, in case you've forgotten

We don't live within the confines of a reality show
Where we can just change the channel when
We don't like the way the plot twists
Real life doesn't work that way
And, this, my friends and my foes,
This is real life

Zoetrope

All we ever say is
Belittling words to
Cease conversation about
Democracy's ability to
Evolve into something stronger
For all the people it represents.
Gold meaning more than it does to
Hold people above the fray
Insisting that we all understand how
Justice can be perverted in order to
King the truth a
Lie in order to
Manipulate all those who
Never stop to think about the
Oppression of those left in
Perpetual opposition to the
Quick to suppress the
Rights of the powerless
Standing in formation
Together to put forth their
Understanding of the world's
Vision of tomorrow's needs
With nothing left when the
Xenophobes take over with their
Yells of hatred ringing through the
Zoetrope of peace we created and they destroyed

Imitation of a Leader

You stood in front of the crowd
Convinced them your imitation
Was the real thing
Laughed as they believed
Every promise you made
Another con in the bag
Never understanding
That leadership isn't manipulation
The leadership you sought
Was a form of servitude
But the word service
Meant so little to you
You never stopped to think
The power you sought
Came with limits
So you stood on the stage
Pretended to be what
You could never be
Convinced the people
Your imitation was real
And there's a real danger
In assuming leadership
When you don't know
How to serve in order to lead

Words on a Sheet of Paper

Words on a sheet of paper
Are only as good as the paper
They're written on
There's nothing binding about
Writing it on paper or
Even signing your name to it
We accept the binds of
Writing it on paper
Agreeing to it on paper
Setting our intentions on paper
But seriously
Lately I've realized
Even the US Constitution is only
Words on paper
Unless… Unless… Unless
We honor the words
We protect the words
We accept the words
For what they are
A promise
A covenant
A contract
That can only be changed
By writing more words on paper
And agreeing that we'll all abide
By them
We become complacent
Thinking we're protected by
Those words on an ancient sheet of paper
So we stop paying attention
We miss the signs

Until those rights are threatened
By the very people who are supposed to protect them
So what does it mean
To have a constitution
When even the highest authorities
Pretend it's only
Words written on paper

Unnatural Results

These words sound so unnatural
Life changing in their importance
Unreal and unbelievable
Like some kind of television show
Without a script
No happy endings here
As the world is torn asunder
By realities diverging
Into unreal dichotomies
Where hate becomes the new norm
Love is left to flounder in its wake
Truth becomes the enemy
Deception is embraced
Changing everything we took for granted
Our safety nets suddenly filled with holes
Leaking out everything we once stood for
A country left to figure out
What they've done to themselves
When all the checks and balances
No longer check or balance
But only acquiesce
Tradition and progress both on the line
As the people stumble to figure out
How to salvage what they destroyed
And that's how we left it
As the world around us burned

Front Door Freedom

Freedom that sneaks in the back door
Offers no liberation for the inhabitants
How can one be free in a life forced into shadows?
If freedom steals another's liberation
Neither can be free
Freedom that shackles another
Imprisons all

Death Weans

Kings and queens
Paupers and peasants
High towers overlooking the greens
Where the streets are filled with fire ants
The power of death weans
The rich and the poor of their rants

High towers overlooking the greens
Where the streets are filled with fire ants
Feasting on magical beans
Shouting unheard cants
The power of death weans
The rich and the poor of their rants

Feasting on magical beans
Shouting unheard cants
Peace covered in dirty sheens
War killing all the plants
The power of death weans
The rich and the poor of their rants

Peace covered in dirty sheens
War killing all the plants
Kings and queens
Paupers and peasants
The power of death weans
The rich and the poor of their rants

Without Equality There is No Freedom

I stood in the crowd
People standing up for what's right
Someone please explain to me
Why do we have to protest inequality?
Why must we beg for our rights?
Why must we demand what's rightfully ours?
Why is it necessary to seek fairness?
We stand in this crowd
We march in the street
We give eloquent speeches
We write convincing arguments
We take to the courts
All in protest of the denial
Of what's guaranteed in the Constitution
Of what amounts to common sense
Of what's in the best interest of us all
Yet, here we stand
With signs proclaiming our rights
And it all seems so depressing
To live in a country that prides itself on liberty
But denies freedom to so many
Without equality there is no freedom
So stand up beside me, please
Understand what we're fighting for
The right to exist as we are
In a world that wants us
To conform to the confines
That deny us freedom through inequality
So here you are
So here I am
Are we equal yet?
Are we free yet?

Because, and I repeat
Without equality there is no freedom
Without equality there is no freedom
Without equality there is no freedom
Without equality there is no freedom
Without equality there is no freedom
Do you get it yet?
No.
Well, I'll say it until you do
Listen closely this time
Without equality there is no freedom
Without equality there is no freedom
Without equality there is no freedom
This fight won't end until you understand
Without equality there is no freedom
Without equality there is no freedom
Without equality there is no freedom
How many times must I say it?
Without equality there is no freedom
Without equality there is no freedom
One more time just so you never forget
Without equality there is no freedom

Without Freedom There is No Equality

I sat in the empty meadow
No one came to sit with me
As we gave the rally cry of freedom
We cheered our own self-righteousness
Like we were in the middle of basketball game
Our team all the way
We are the champions
The champions of the world
We proudly exclaimed
Everyone else should follow our lead
We know
What's in the best interest of us all
Yet, here I sit
Wondering how we think we're free
When we deny so many equality
There is no freedom when we oppress
There is no freedom when we hate
There is no freedom when we possess
You tell me about this utopia
That represents the world you think exists
But I can't find it
It's a fantasy you've concocted to survive
We must convince ourselves
We are the arbiters of freedom
Even as we deny so many equality
So here you are
So here I am
Are we equal yet?
Are we free yet?
Because, and I repeat
Without freedom there is no equality
Without freedom there is no equality

Without freedom there is no equality
Without freedom there is no equality
Do you get it yet?
No.
Well, I'll say it until you do
Listen closely this time
Without freedom there is no equality
Without freedom there is no equality
Without freedom there is no equality
This fight won't end until you understand
Without freedom there is no equality
Without freedom there is no equality
Without freedom there is no equality
How many times must I say it?
Without freedom there is no equality
Without freedom there is no equality
One more time just so you never forget
Without freedom there is no equality

The Loss We Found

Numbed to the world
Progressing quite fluidly
Smiles adorning our faces
Laughter easily escaping our lips
We were sure we'd found the answer
To fix all the pain we'd encountered
Finally, we were on our way to seeing
Our fellow Earthlings with compassion
We would finally embrace
Our myriad contributions
We could finally celebrate
Our similarities and differences
We could see the truth
Within each of our lives
And, then hatred spewed forth
Flooding all the good around us
Taking over the unity we'd found
Creating rivers between us
That would dry into empty gulches
You on one side
Me on the other
Trying desperately to bridge these canyons
Above turbulent waters
As the rain poured burning us like acid
Stripping away the connection we'd made
The forest around us growing darker each minute
As lightning flashed and thunder roared above
We looked at all those advances we'd made
Disappearing beneath the roaring waves
Crashing into boulders and smashing to bits
As we shouted into the wind

For all the gains to be protected
Even as they were undone
Leaving us with losses
We'd need to find
In order to recover
The work of yesterday
Obliterated by the hate of today
Leaving us with tomorrow to start again
Because no matter how much we've lost
We'll find the strength to rise again
We'll find the compassion to bridge the gaps
We'll find the way to gain back the loss

Whitewashing History

Whitewashing history
Romanticizing atrocities committed
Creating a world where the heroes
Always look just like us
Refusing to see beyond our narrative
The narrative we create to hide the truth

Tired of FUD

I don't know about you
But I'm tired
I'm so very tired of
The fear
The uncertainty
The doubt
Woven into our lives
It exhausts me
I'm so tired
Of people excusing hate
Because they can't let go of
The fear
The uncertainty
The doubt
That they're told will protect them
From unseen, unheard, untouched enemies
There's nothing left in a world where
The fear
The uncertainty
The doubt
Rule the world
I refuse to accept your fear
I refuse to accept your uncertainty
I refuse to accept your doubt
There to manipulate me
Into turning my back on the vulnerable
I've been vulnerable
I've been hungry
I've been scared
I am everything you hate
I am strong and vulnerable

I am resilient and honest
I am accepting and compassionate
I value unity over division
I value life over borders
I value love over hate
So you can keep
The fear
The uncertainty
The doubt
You spew at the top of your lungs
To rile up hatred and divisiveness
I don't need it
The world I live in
Isn't filled with monsters
Just because you say it is
No, I look at the hated
And I see friends I haven't met yet
I see faces in need of a smile
I see lives in need of a change
I see possibility
I see a future
Filled with hope and promise
That someday your
Fear
Uncertainty
Doubt
Will burn to ashes in fires of change

I Won't Let You Steal My Joy

This
This
This
Is my joy
I won't let you steal my joy
It is mine
And I will cling to it
No, you don't get to steal my joy
That victory I can deny you
You might make me fight
For everything I hold dear
But I will fight with joy and grit
Determination and willpower
I will smile when I feel like it
I will frown when I feel like it
But, this, oh, this is my joy
And you can't steal it
You can't destroy it
You might take my right to speak
But I will shout from behind my gag
You might take my right to assemble
But I will gather together a wall you can't break
You might take everything I own
But I will still have me
You might seek to destroy me
Because you don't like my lifestyle
Or my skin color
Or my gender identification
Or my sexual orientation
Or my hippie attitude
Or my insistence on science

Or my choice of religion
Or my choice of rejection of religion
Or my income, or lack thereof
Oh, you might take away my freedom
But I will go down fighting
And I will fight with every ounce of love
I can find it this world
Because all those people you hate
I love just because they exist
Nothing more
I don't need them to earn my love
I don't need them to prove themselves worthy
I don't need them to fit some arbitrary mold
No, I just see their humanity
And that's enough to know
Love must conquer hate
Or else there's nothing left to live for
So when you tell me
How miserable my wonderful life is
I want to laugh in your face
You want me to be miserable
You want me to turn on my fellow human beings
You want me to spread hate and divisiveness
I refuse to play along
I will stand here in my joy
Seeing my life for all its magnificence
Hearing my life for all its melody
Feeling my life for all its sensuality
Smelling my life for all its perfume
Tasting my life for all its lusciousness
Oh, see, I worked too damn hard
To find this joy
That comes from
Living from a place of love

As hard as the road ahead might be
The one thing I refuse to do is
Let you
Steal my precious joy

Unstop the Drain

This drain we've created
Is so stopped up
The world has become putrid
We lob in a little greed
We toss in a little hatred
We throw in a bit of violence
We sneak in a bit of dishonesty
We pitch in a little fear
We stir it all around
And wait for something good to manifest
Someone pulls the plug
But nothing drains out
We've stopped up the pipes
With so much divisiveness
Nothing can drain out
No matter how much love and compassion
You and I apply to flush out the drain
The sewer gases overwhelm us
We find ourselves wallowing in
Everything we wish to change
But, one of these days, we will find
Just the right pipe snake
To clear this clog
And drain away everything the haters built
So we can replace it with a foundation
Of love
Of acceptance
Of compassion
Of understanding
Of unity

Of justice
Of truth
Of hope
That will keep the drain free and clear
To wash away all the putridity
Just you wait and see

Night Within a Day

The moon covers the sun
Brings a night within a day
Where the sky above darkens
Where the sun and the moon quiver
We're standing in the middle
Of our own eclipse
Tyranny tries to block democracy
But democracy shines around the edges
Of the black hole of tyranny
Leaving us grasping to hold onto those shreds of light
Democracy behind the moon peeking around the edges
Determined to shine again
Telling tyranny to be on its way
To find another place to dwell
As you and I march in the streets
As you and I stand up for love
As you and I stand against hate
As you and I search for hope
As you and I reach around tyranny to grasp the light
We know is ours if we just hold tight
Waiting for tyranny to move on
So democracy can shine brighter than ever
Our only hope being that
Tyranny eclipsing democracy
Is only
Passing through
Like a night within a day

Our System

We are all part of this system
Pulling and pushing
Wishing and wanting
Loving and hating
We put in our time
We punch out our productivity
Playing our roles
Cogs in the wheels
Of this system
Into which we're born
Lies that prime us
To believe more lies
Training us to accept
What others tell us we are
What others tell us we aren't
What others tell us to be
We pay our dues
We give lives
We scream loyalty
Even as we're stripped
Of everything we think
Of everything we desire
Of everything we know
Told time and again
Thinking is a sign of disloyalty
You don't know what you know
Someone else will save you
The leaders know your life better than you
Follow the party line
Don't argue

Don't think
Don't resist
Play your role
Feed the system
Accept the lies
Never question
Never question
Never question
If you do
Our system just might fail
But is it our system
Or
Their system
Designed to keep us
Obedient, ignorant, loyal

Spoken with Authority

You spoke with such authority
Your lies sounded like scientific fact
You never stuttered a single word
Bloviating for hours on end
Never pausing long enough
For anyone to present you with facts
No one bothers to argue with you
You wear them down
With your nonstop chatter
Spoken with such conviction
Never a doubt inflicting your authoritative voice
Just because no one bothers to argue
Doesn't mean they believe you
Just because they nod their heads
Doesn't mean they're even listening
Just because they smile
Doesn't mean anyone takes you seriously
So keep speaking
Waste your words
On ears that have closed to your lies
Spoken with such strong authority

Nothing Ever Changes

We go through this cycle
Time and again
Wash, rinse, repeat
How many times can we do this?
Fighting the good fight
Being on the right side of history
Seeing the truth
Embracing one another
Fighting against those who discriminate
Standing tall in the face of hatred
Misogyny, racism, fascism
Following your rules
So you can feel free
By imprisoning others
In roles they weren't mean to play
Just to keep your conventional world in place
Never stopping long enough to see
The value in those who are different than you
How bringing together
People, culture, ideas
Only expands our knowledge
Only offers new solutions
Only shows us just how alike we are
But, oh, we've been fighting this fight
Since before my birth
So, sometimes, as much progress as we make
It really, truly seems
Nothing ever really changes
But, my friend, we can do this
Whether you're from here or there or wherever

The battle we fight against those who stand
In the way of change
Is a battle we can't afford to lose
A battle for love
A battle of love
A battle with love
We will fight until the bitter end
And we will find the change
That unites and unifies
We will reach a day when equality is real
We will love without hesitation
And if nothing changes in my lifetime
The next generation will fight the good fight
Even when it feels like
Nothing ever really changes…

Rabid Dogs

You welcomed me
Into your pack
So we could band together
To break down the web of corruption
The rabid dog frothed at the mouth
Spewing the hatred from deep within
Words defying all logic
But spreading the vitriol
Gift wrapped in promises to clean the rabies
Dripping from his mouth with every word
Until all the lapdogs began to froth
In unison
Feeding the infected, infectious dog's wrath
We stood on the outside
Confident we'd never have to mobilize
Because we believed logic would rule the day
Yet here we stand
The rabid dog ready to take us all down
So we can no longer trust the system to work
We have to be vigilant
We have to fight back
We have to stand strong
Creating a web of cooperation
Between packs of love
So we can band together against the hate
To stop the frothing dog in its tracks
Give logic a foothold again
We have to remember
Freedom begins with love
But, a rabid dog must be stopped
Before it destroys everything in its path

Praising the Unpraiseworthy

Bow your head
Heap words of adulation
Never question the praise you give
We're often encouraged to
Praise the unworthy
And
Condemn the worthy
Yet
So often the person deemed unworthy
In the present
History finds the most worthy
Standing up for equality
Has long been a cause for condemnation
Labeled with unkind labels
Insults meant to silence and protect the status quo
Yet when someone calls me a
Social justice warrior
I see it as high praise
Even as I hear the hate dripping from their tongue
Social justice is worth fighting for
Seeking equality for all is worth marching for
Bringing compassion to society is worth pursuing
Promoting unity is worth the taunts
So go ahead
Lob your insults my way
I'm a social justice warrior snowflake
Ready to blow a blizzard around your hate
With my love
And someday I'll be the one praised by history
And, you, well, you'll be left to explain
Why you fought against equality

Why you demonized social justice
Why you chose hate over love
Yet, I'll have to be condemned today
While you're praised by the haters
So that I can help create a better future for us all
Go ahead, praise the unworthy
I don't need your praise
To do the right thing

Con Job Exposed

You thought you could con me
Seduce me with toxic words
I felt your intentions rub against my skin
As you tried to pass me from behind
Anger made my face flush
But I saw through every oxymoron you shared
Your lies grew through each telling
Drowning me in a world of toxicity
Pushing me away from your rub
I rushed past your con job
Ready to flush you right out of my life
And therein lies the ultimate oxymoron
Your attempt to deceive me
Exposed you for the con man you are

Shall We Talk of War

Shall we talk of war
The battles you never fought
The losses you never felt
The truth you never believed
The peace you never sought

Shall we talk of war
The bombs you never dropped
The missiles you never launched
The reality you never accepted
The peace you never sought

Shall we talk of war
The blood you never shed
The torture you never endured
The waking nightmares you never dreamed
The peace you never sought

Shall we talk of war
The peace you never sought

Battle Me Now

We stood on opposite sides
Of every issue
Never giving an inch
Waiting for the opening
To drive in a wedge
To make a point
To prove the other wrong
Not seeking understanding
Not seeking connection
Not seeking truth
We each only wanted to be right
So we stood on opposite sides
Armed and dangerous
Ready to battle to the death
Over some perception
Based on belief
Ignoring all the facts
As the world around us crashed
On our heads
But, oh, we were determined
To prove our side was right
You and me on opposite sides
Of every issue
Never giving an inch
Daring the other into battle
Vowing to fight to the death
While the powerful watched
Us tear each other apart
Laughing as our division grew
Alongside their bank accounts
Keeping us in battle

Insured we'd never rise up together
Linking arms and seeing our future
Depended on us setting down our arms
Declaring the battle against each other over
Turning our fight to the greed and corruption
That destroyed the world around us

Fighting Amongst Ourselves

We stand in alliance
In our defiance
Yet we can't allow
Each other a single foul
Calling out every mistake
Even when the accusation is fake
We suffer blowback
From our blue on blue contact
As we arm ourselves against
Those within our own midst
We give ammunition
To our opposition
They laugh at their own fraud
As we form a circular firing squad
Why let them take us down
When we can do the dirty work for the clown
Let's stop this self-destruction
Turning instead to reconstruction
Come hold my hand
We'll fight to understand
Holding up the truth to the light
Never giving up the fight
Embracing our imperfection
Stopping these calls for perfection
Hold their feet to the ice
Because we have the goals to entice
So next time they destroy our rights
Remind them we don't buy their frights

Oh, no, we will no longer
Buy their contract

To blue on blue contact

Oh no, we will no longer
Ride roughshod
To embrace a circular firing squad

United in our quest
To create a future progressed

Kindness Lost

Spouting insults
Lobbing threats
Hiding behind a keyboard
Anonymous posts
Words one would never
Have the courage to say
Face to face
Has technology
Desensitized us
To the point
We no longer
Have any compassion
Have we lost all respect?
Have we lost all sense of decency?
Would a little kindness kill us?

Take Him at His Word

You said
Take him at his word
But when I pointed out
The words you didn't like
Your tune changed
Not those words
He didn't mean those words
But he said them
We either have to take him
At all his words
Or none of his words
Then we have to hold him accountable
Which of those words are true?
Which of those words are lies?
We'll find out, won't we?
It might be too late to save ourselves
But we will find out
When the words become actions
Or the words are betrayed by actions
When the contradictions are resolved
And action is taken
Then what?
Will it be too late to fix the damage?
Amazing how the words I believe
And the words you believe
Differ so greatly when we say
Take him at his word

Bless Your Heart

I know you believed
Those words you so
Desperately want to hear
They were spoken with
Such passion
They resonated with your pain
You dismissed what
Seemed over the top
You wanted someone, anyone
To make your life better
So you bought the
Fool's gold
That glittered
So brightly it blinded you
Never bothering to see
The scapegoat offered
Was no threat to you
The message convoluted
The chaos created
The contradictory promises
Hyperbole filling the voids
To pump up the sentiment
Words that never reflected reality
And still you refuse to see
As you cling to what will never be
Bless your heart
Bless your ever-loving heart
Bless your poor naïve heart

Freedom Fights Greed

There's a fragility
To this freedom
We take for granted
With thoughts that
We're somehow immune
To the forces that influence
So we trudge along
Believing leaders care
About our interests
While they fill their pockets
Until they overflow
While they stuff in more and more
Only spending to buy more money
Unwilling to pay workers their worth
Pretending like those who create
Aren't the ones who produce
Ignoring the destruction they wrought
On the world where they live
Seeing people as expenses
Instead of investments
Treating the world like it owes them
Even though they have more than
They can ever spend
Always wanting more
Because power comes from money
Money brings more power
Feeding their greed
Until they can't see beyond
Money, money, money
Power, power, power
Corruption rules our lives

And we are expected to
Beg for more corruption
In the hopes some crumbs
Might fall from the hems
Of those stomping on our heads
What if… what if… what if…
We all stop offering up our heads
We all stop thanking those who stomp on us
We all stop buying into the paradigm
What if… what if… what if…
We see our own worth
Stop allowing consumerism to give us
A false sense of power
To keep feeding the powerful and the rich
What if… what if… what if
We stand up and speak
We refuse to sit down and shut up
We insist on being paid our worth
We insist on the power of the people
We stand up for each other
We insist on equality for all
We live love in the face of hate
We refuse to be divided
We fight to preserve our world
What if… what if… what if…

Whispered in An Empty Room

There are words
Whispered in an empty room
To no one who will ever hear
The silence we left in the recesses
Where words echoed to nothing
Sliding into oblivion
For the lack of anyone to hear them
Words, you wish didn't need whispered
Or shouted or even thought
As another man, woman, child lays dying
In the cold hard arms of a concrete jungle
Where to live is to be silenced
Whenever one dares start a conversation
Speaking words no one wants to hear
Some who wish they weren't necessary
Others who deem them unnecessary
A fight to the end
Where a single word whispered
Sparks a debate that rages
Between those who live the experience
And those who analyze the experience
When will we understand to be heard
Takes both the words spoken
And the ear willing to hear
One without the other is just
Noise lost in too much silence
Words whispered in an empty room
Reverberating off the walls
Only to be heard by the speaker
As a final breath for justice exhales

Quietude

Quiet settles in
Drowning out the chaos
Created by the chatter
Intent on keeping communication dead
Or at least sedated
My brain screamed for me to stop
Listening to the noise
Put an end to the spiraling negativity
Hate loves to spread
So I turned off the source
Listened to the quiet in the wind
All the chatter does nothing to solve the problem
It only pulls us all into a vortex
Where no one hears the words
Nothing ever changes
We all give up
Because to give a damn
Eats away our ability to converse intelligently
So keep your chatter, keep your chaos
Give me intelligent discourse
Then maybe we will see each other as human
Allowing us to reach for true solutions
Rather than just shouting to be heard
Above the chaos intended to make things worse
So as I retreat into quiet
Don't see defeat
I'm only waiting out your chaos
Until the day you wear yourself out
Then, maybe, just maybe, we can have a real conversation

Erasing the Borders

I took the map
Stared at all the lines
Dividing humanity
Driving a wedge between us
Standing on either side
Creating artificial differences
Differences determined by
Borders drawn on a map
I stared at those borders
Creating so many problems
What if... what if... what if
I took my little eraser
Removed all those artificial borders
So we could no longer keep others out
For the crime of being born within the wrong borders
So we could no longer kill others
For the crime of being born within the wrong borders
So we could no longer hate others
For the crime of being born within the wrong borders
Because when it comes down to it
Everyone thinks someone's borders are the wrong borders
What if... what if... what if
I picked up an eraser
Began to erase the dividing lines
We tell ourselves make us different
We tell ourselves make us good
We tell ourselves make the other bad
Artificial borders drawn on a map
I wonder if your god, or your god, or your gods
Watch us all dividing ourselves and laughs or cries
At our artificial borders

Thinking
"It's all my territory, assholes."
"Those people you hate are mine, too, assholes."
"Who do you think you are, assholes?"
But then again, maybe your god, your god, or your gods
Are just as selfish, shallow, and self-serving
As we all are in our quest to preserve
Our artificial borders
To bolster our artificial loyalty
To excuse our artificial hatred
To justify our artificial beliefs
In order to ignore the reality
Of very real violence
Of very real greed
Of very real pain inflicted
If I erased those borders
Could we see each other's humanity?
Could we feel each other's pain?
Could we find a way to connect?
As I erased border after border
I felt the futility of the effort
People cling to their borders
Because their borders define their identities
How can we see beyond the borders
When we can't even see beyond our selves?

Experienced at Saying Nothing

Experienced at saying nothing
With a slew of words
A smile charmingly enticing
The next victim
To blindly follow words
That divide the herd
Culling the disobedient
Who ruminate on facts
Instead of fears
Driving power
To those who wish
To destroy rather than build
Such experience leads to blackholes
Of hatred
That crush all possibility
Of sunshine to cleanse
The darkness
Those experienced at saying nothing
Must be forced to say something
Because power without substance
Wrenches peace into chaos

Carefully Crafted Careless Words

These damages you inflict
With your carefully crafted careless words
Don't hurt any less because
You claim they're your beliefs
Your hateful beliefs aren't sacrosanct
And no less hateful because you hide behind religion
Beliefs aren't facts no matter how strongly you believe them
Repeating them ad nauseum doesn't make them any more true
Beliefs have consequences, particularly when they inflict harm
Understand that just because you claim to only be being honest
Doesn't absolve you from guilt when you speak harmful words
Spreading hate, spreading discord, spreading disinformation
Feigning wide-eyed innocence and claiming your words shouldn't hurt
After all they're only your deeply held beliefs
Seriously doesn't mean you don't inflict any damage
Own the damage you inflict and be ready for the consequences
Of your carefully crafted careless words

Changing the World

Floating in nostalgia
Looking down on yesterday
Forgetting what today offers
Releasing dreams of the future
Yesterday held the promise
Of what we thought could be.
Brash and loud and optimistic
We had no doubt our efforts
Would change the world
We would stand together
Unite the world
So everyone could see
The detriment of hatred
We would be the shining example
Of what happens when two worlds combine
We would show the whole world
That our dreams could bring us all to peace
We'd no longer need war or violence or divisiveness.
Our dreams would put an end to all
The unwarranted hatred our ancestors clung to
Because we could see the path forward
We would meet each other on equal footing
Forge forward on ground fertile for compassion
We would celebrate our diversity
We would bond over our similarities
We would prove to those who came before
We could make the complex simple
Because we heard the cries asking us
To judge each other on our character and actions
Not our skin color, religion, or gender
We heard the cries begging us

To accept each other based on our hearts and minds
Not on our sexuality, ethnic background, or clothing
We knew as we cloaked ourselves in righteous indignation
We were the generation to end all the ignorance that came before
We would solve the world's problems
Like a soda commercial singing about smiling
Or a group of pop singers singing about poverty
Or a poet writing about how much we have in common
We would be the ones to take all those words to heart
We would be the generation to learn from others' mistakes
We would be the ones who would unite the world in peace
In spite of the avarice, disdain, and vitriol we saw in prior generations
We swore we would be different
And now decades later we gear up to make our voices heard
Because we were too complacent
That we could learn from their mistakes
And create a world based on love, compassion, and understanding
We thought
The protests have been done
The sweat has been shed
The tears have been cried
The marches have been marched
The truth is now accepted
But, oh, how wrong we were
So I stand beside my brothers and sisters
My fellow Earthlings
And I cry into the wind
Scream into the night
Stand shoulder to shoulder
With a person a stranger has declared enemy
Let love pour from my heart
See the humanity in the eyes of the terrified
Understand that when hate rules the day
The terrorist takes on the form of the once protector

But I refuse to be scared, or at least to show my fear
For when they come for my brother or my sister
Of another background
They come for me, too…

Bedfellows: Conformity and Resistance

The drip of words
We dribble across the world
Holding us hostage to expectation
As the world turns a blind eye
To the pain it inflicts
In an insatiable thirst for hunger
We search for answers
To bring those without power
Into the conversation
While those in power
Seek to shut us all up
No words that don't conform
Even when we're protesting conformity
Conform to my resistance
We shout from the streets
Wondering why everyone can't see
What we see
Marching toward equality
I won't back down, not today, not tomorrow
This world needs more people
Who question authority
I'm sure of that
We need to see the humanity
In you, in me, in her, in him
In the world around us
We need to see the value
Of the soil, the water, the trees
That make up the world around us
We need to understand
We are but one spoke in the wheel
That keeps this cycle going

So how do we engage the future
We need to step into to save
The present as we see it today
From the past harm we inflicted
Oh, but how do we do it
When conformity and resistance
Seem to be such passionate bedfellows

Intellectual Boredom Run Amok

I don't have time
To dissect the unimportant
To indulge your ridiculous whims
To listen to you pontificate
Just to feel self-important
I don't have the energy
To worry about artificial labels
Designed to inflate egos
Or denigrate another person
I'm too busy trying to live a life of value
To be so worried that someone might get credit
For something that doesn't fit into a narrow box
How incredibly insecure one must be
To feel a need to worry about such trivial things
As whether or not every box is checked off
To meet the conventional definition of this label or that
If you have that much time on your hands
Maybe just maybe you could put it toward something
That will make the world a better place
For all its inhabitants
Somehow the harder you try to convince others
Just how intellectually elite you are
The less we believe you
Eyes roll every time you speak
People cease to discuss anything with you
Because all you do is
Pontificate to prove something
You don't even believe yourself
And really all we want to say is
I disengage not because you're right
But because the whole artificial debate

Bores holes of boredom through our skulls

Bells of History

We stood below the campanile
Listened to the bells
That rang a story we didn't understand
A history long forgotten to all those around us
The tears of oppression ringing through the air
A past of hatred and vitriol echoing behind
The hope and peace of the sweet sound
Of bells ringing as the sun rose
Streaks of red, orange, yellow
Glowing off the white campanile
Like a bleeding halo
Crowning a society seeking unity
In the face of deep division
I closed my eyes
Let the bells give my feet rhythm
On a cold morning
Stepping forward in a march
Straight into the future
Where the bells will celebrate
While never forgetting the struggle
Of those who gave us hope
When the bells rang at sunset
Because we knew there would be another sunrise
Lighting up the campanile
As the bells rang the story
Determined to make us understand
The story we all needed to hear

Look or See

You look at me
I look at you
We look
But do we see
A smile here
A frown there
A past untold
A future unwritten
A present unshared
Words not spoken
Amid assumptions
We take a peek
At the surface
Seeing the façade
Believing the stories
We tell ourselves
About one another
As long as we're quiet
Nothing challenges imagination
As soon as we speak
We might just see
Really see each other
But do you want to
Really see me
But do I want to
Really see you
Oh, we look and look and look
But when it comes time to
See, we avoid eye contact
We avoid anything that challenges
Us to look beyond what we believe

So shall we look or shall we see

Privilege

I crashed through your defenses
Reaching into your perfect little life
Making you think about all those things
You didn't want to consider
Because if you didn't think them
Somehow, they didn't matter
You could go about your life
Ignoring all the pain
Of those who could easily be you
If you'd been born
In a different skin
In a different body
In a different place
No, you never stopped to see yourself
In the eyes of another
Because a life of privilege
Is so much easier to accept
Than to see yourself through another's eyes
To see you might be the expression
Of everything you claim to despise
As you walk through your life
Wearing your privilege like a warm cloak
Shutting out the cold wind
Protecting you from the falling snow
Shielding you from the dark of night
Lighting the path in front of you
As it reflects off all those you step on to reach the moon
Your oblivion oozing from your pours like sweat
Dripping on the backs of those who hold you aloft
And, yet, your greed can never be quenched
As you steal the cloaks of all those around you

Just because you can
Taking privilege from the unprivileged
And telling them to thank you for it
As you promise them licking your hem
Will elevate them above others
Giving them faux privilege as unearned as yours
Then laughing when they try to exercise the promised privilege
Because your power is in keeping them begging
For the crumbs you only tease

Independence

Is this independence?
You look offended
It's a real question
I'm not sure I recognize it
This doesn't feel like independence
Oppression of another is never independence
Imprisonment of the innocent is never independence
Stoking fear to keep people in line is never independence
So tell me again how this rates as independence.
I don't see it
Hate and vitriol are never independence
So I ask you again is this independence
When your freedom comes on the backs of another
How is that independence?
When your independence leaves boot marks on others' necks
How is that independence?
When your independence relies on another's enslavement
How is that independence?
When your independence denies others the rights you take for granted
How is that independence?
The fantasy of independence is romantic
The reality of independence feels much more like oppression
But go ahead
Light up the sky with pollution
To prove how much you love the country
You're hell bent on destroying
Because without equality for all
There is no independence for any

Violence Never Begets Peace

I smile as your dagger
Hits that spot right where
The blood flows the strongest
Bleeding my pain all over
Your pristine pearl handle
With words placed so carefully
To destroy the strength I
So carefully cultivated
Out of the vulnerability
You used as a weapon
To land your blows
In this fragilely constructed being
That you can't see as real
Only as a place for your hatred to hit
Its mark
Giving you a rush of superiority
As you criticize me for my existence
That doesn't conform to yours
Telling me I'm unworthy of life
Simply because I'm not just like you
When I feel the dagger's point
Separate the skin beneath it
I know the cut you make
Destroys you more than me
But that doesn't make it hurt any less
As I seek the support of a stranger
Who promises to protect me
From your dagger
Only to feel your dagger
Lash out against the stranger, too
So you spill the blood of strength

Into the streets so you can feel superior
While those who stand as different
Hold each other's hands and promise
Strangers though we might be
We will find a way to ebb this flow
We fill find a way to be who we are
The blood of vulnerability will unite us
As your dagger seeks to untie us
We won't allow you to destroy
The very thing that makes us strong
Our diversity bonded in blood and water and earth
Stands up to your hate
Our wounds are healed by love
Our scars evidence of our solutions
Our blood evidence we are alive
So we'll stand arm in arm unarmed
As you plow forth with your arms
Trying to prove your superiority
In a world where equality frightens you
Our hearts, our blood, our minds
Joined in a celebration of Earthlings
Who see the value in sharing our
Similarities and our differences
Because as we come together
We find peace never comes
At the end of a weapon

Important Insignificance

Ignoble, ignorant idol
Fancying one's self iconic
Standing in another's spotlight
Unaware of casting shadows
Over every pertinent poise
Of poignant prose
Translated to tyranny
In words meant to deceive
Worshipped by those who
Couldn't be bothered to think
Lauded by those who
Couldn't be bothered to feel
Lionized by those who
Couldn't be bothered to hear
Lacking compassion for any
Who didn't reflect the desired image
Back into a crowd where vitriol ruled
Until the day control faltered
Leaving the ignorant idol
Denying the damage committed
By exalting one's self into a place
Of faux significance
The hungry ego starving for attention
To prove all the stories in one's head
Never stopping to understand the
Incredible insignificance
Of declaring unearned importance

Forward, Backward, Onward

This precipice where we stand
Looking forward hand-in-hand

Waiting for the last star to rise
So we can find a way to stop the cries

Echoes of history floating through word after word
Shouted by those who seed discord

Among those who would seek to love
Without the need to sacrifice a dove

Standing steadfast looking into the future
Knowing this divide won't be fixed with a suture

Hate spilling from the lips of pale faces
Seeking to erase equality from all places

Footprints of fear stomp on our rights
Forcing hate into spotlights

So we look backward hand-in-hand
From this precipice where we stand

Wondering if the fall
Will kill us all

Knowing the only choice is to leap
Into the abyss below as we try to keep

Our sanity in the loss of compassion

That we should never seek to ration

Your deception leaves stains
That can't be washed away by rains

So from the precipice where we still stand
We look onward hand-in-hand

I'm Still Here

I'm still here
No matter what you say
You can't change that
You might ignore my presence
You might make up excuses
You might try to pretend
But every time you look
My presence remains
I stood tall as you raged
I stared straight ahead until you blinked
Blow after blow landed on its mark
Lies reverberated through the air
You never once saw your role
In all that destroyed the world around us
Hate and vitriol spewing from your cursed lips
Poisoning all those within hearing distance
Drowning the good
Pretending you were mightier than others
After all the rhetoric died down
I simply whispered
I'm still here
And off you raged again…
But I refuse to be moved
I refuse to cower beneath your hate
I refuse to be silenced
So every time you pause
I'm going to whisper
I'm still here…
I'm still here…
I'm still here…

Devoted to a Mistake

Sometimes a mistake feels so right
We dive in without looking below the surface
Without testing what lies below the shiny reflection
Diving into depths we cannot possibly fathom
Reaching for some elusive footing
As we flounder in the unswimmable
Longing to break back through the surface
To the light we see as our salvation
Drowning in despair
Gasping for liberation
Sinking deeper into the mistake
Until we forget the mistake is a mistake
Digging deeper into the mistake
Defending our position
Unwilling to grasp the lifeline
That would allow us to correct
The mistake we cling to with such devotion

Complicit

I am complicit
In this moment
We share
I engage fully
With a smile
Accompanied by
A heavy heart
Life pulls us
In opposite directions
Making our differences shine
While our similarities drown
In the truth of this moment
Where chaos dictates
Your moves and mine
As we reach for something simple
That shouldn't cause grief
Yet somehow
This moment that feels so right
Brings up so much that is wrong
And we ache for a connection
We can't find in a world tipping
Off its axis
Leaving us flailing in the dream
Of what we thought we were
Or at least the fantasy of
What we thought we could become
Yet we talk and talk
We walk and walk
We seek and seek
This mire of love and hate
Drowning us in its wake

As we stand and promise
I won't betray you
I won't betray my principles
I won't betray my promises
And yet we move forward into
A day where our goals are
Uncertain of themselves
And all we know is that
This tangled mess we've created
Leaves us all
Complicit in the world we inhabit

Stable Full of Lies

Therein lies the lie
The truth nowhere to be found
Your lips spew forth words
That have no bearing in reality
If only your nose would grow like Pinocchio's
So we could see, hell, so I could've seen, the lie
Before the damage it dumped on me
All the lies shoveled deeper than
A full stable left uncleaned
All the manure building up
Making it hard to walk through the barn
The stench unbearable
Knee deep in horseshit, bullshit, pigshit
Oh, the lies that bury the truth
Like a discarded treasure
Only to be found
After a lifetime of shoveling
The lies out of our hearts
So we can find a truth
To dispel the lies
And free us all

Broken Words

You shared your words
They broke before my eyes
As I read them
Heard them in your voice
Coming from my memory
The words you said
Shocking my system
What did I miss?
Is this who you always were?
This hate permeating words
You deny are hateful
How can you not see?
How can you not feel?
Just how broken your words are
Tears fill my eyes as I listen
Your words, though not about me
Your words, though not to me
Your words, though not for me
Break my heart
Because they reveal
You are not who I thought you were

Enemies

I feel you
Reaching for me
From a million miles away
In your own little world
Just like I'm in mine
Occasionally breaking through the bubble
To connect for just long enough to remember
There's more to both our lives
Than the day to day moments
Lost in the mundane minutiae
Pretending this move or that move
Will make a difference in the larger world
Outside all these little bubbles where we hide
Seeking to connect with hearts that are open
But finding minds that are closed
Pain waltzes between the words spoken
Shifting our sense of connection to suspicion
Because our differences make us enemies
Even though we long to be friends
I reach up to burst my bubble
Only to find you've strengthened yours
So I retreat back inside mine
Adding another layer of armor
We shout at each other
Trying to be heard in the chaotic chimes
We can't quiet
In a world losing its mind
In search of a drama
To keep us from facing the numbness
We've been sleepwalking toward
This thing that angers you

This thing that saddens me
This thing that keeps us fighting
This thing that keeps us divided
What if we stopped letting
Someone else tell us
We should be enemies
And instead put down our guns
Talked to each other like friends, or even strangers
What if....
What if...
What if...
I'm not your enemy
You're not my enemy
But the enemy is the one telling us
We should be enemies...

Prickly

You were so prickly
You found a reason
To attack the world
To try to soothe your prickles
Sending explosives to those
You saw as enemy
Those defined by someone else
As enemy
You wanted to blow up everything
Because your hackles were up
You were scared of losing
What you never had
So scared the world was changing
Leaving you behind
Because you refuse to change
So you want to stop all progress
Blowing up the world
Blowing up the country
Blowing up your enemy
Won't give you the relief you want
No, it won't
Instead you'll find yourself
Sitting behind bars
Stuck in time
While the rest of us
Defeat your agenda
And move forward
To a place of equality, love, compassion
We won't let your hate destroy us

When They Own You

When they own you
What do you have left?
Your life becomes lost
In a web woven to eat you alive
The words they speak
Become the gospel you can't question
The lies you're fed
Slowly poison your existence
Killing you with every syllable
While you lap them up
Like you're dying of thirst
No nourishment to be found
Keeps you addicted to the sound
Of the voices taunting you every time
You dare step out of line
Trying to take the antidote with a dose of truth
The lies running through your veins
Infecting you with every utterance that confirms
What you know isn't true but dare not question
You hide the antidote in the recesses of your mind
Trying to make sense of the existence you inhabit
Where truth no longer seems to matter
Knowing you'll die if you keep swallowing the lies
Forced into every bite you eat, every breath you breathe
Standing next to a whispering truth tugging at your heart
To jump in front of the next bullet aimed at a truth seeker
Knowing that if you stay silent
You allow the poison to spread
But fearing if you open your mouth
The hatred will pierce your heart
Leaving you doubting every truth you hear

Even as the lies refuse to die
How can the truth live
When they own you
Heart, soul, and mind...

Scorching Words

Your words scorched the hearts
They infiltrated as they flew
Mindlessly through the air
The damage you caused
Breaking the backs of people
Who never did you any harm
You manipulated them to
Suppress themselves
So you could bathe in power
The same power you used
To scorch the people you conned
Who prostrated themselves before you
Wallowing in the pain and sorrow
You promised to alleviate
Only to use it against them
In the name of greed
And the rest of us
The ones you couldn't fool
Resisted your scorching words
Knowing that you'll wither away
Inside your own hatred and greed
As we change the narrative
So truth and justice can prevail
Leaving your corruption in ashes

Underneath

Underneath the lies
Underneath the division
Underneath the beliefs
Underneath the manipulation
Underneath the blind loyalty
Underneath the greed
Underneath the judgment
Underneath it all
What do you find underneath?
When you look in your heart?
When you look in your soul?
Do you ever look
Underneath
To see the humanity in another?
Do you ever look
Underneath
To see the pain in another's eyes?
Do you ever look
Underneath
To find the humility to change
The system that hurts so many
Do you ever look
Underneath
To see the love that unites?
Do you ever look
Underneath
To find the connection
To another?
Do you ever look
Underneath
To find the peace

Born from compassion?
Because I have to believe
That if we look
Underneath
We can find the connection
We can find the compassion
We can find the love
We can find the way to cultivate
Peace
But we have to start by looking
Underneath
The manipulation that keeps us in chaos
Tell me
If peace begins in each of our hearts
How do we nurture it so it will thrive?
Peace is about so much more than ending war
Peace begins and ends with us
Living love and compassion for our fellow Earthlings…

Bullets Don't Discriminate

When the bullet hits
It doesn't ask
Are you conservative?
Are you liberal?
Are you straight?
Are you gay?
Are you female?
Are you male?
Are you transgender?
Are you white?
Are you black?
Are you American?
Are you…
No, the bullet doesn't care
It strikes with the same force
No matter whom you love
No matter where you find joy
No matter what you believe
No matter why you exist
No, the bullet doesn't care
It glides through the air
Searching for its target
Ready to kill with a single touch
No discrimination in its heart
It can't feel what the shooter feels
But it can deliver the shooter's hate
Right into the heart of love
When that hate explodes
All it leaves in its wake
Is the destruction of the
Indiscriminate bullet

Pray for Your Prey

We offer thoughts and prayers
To those who've suffered distress
At the end of a gun
While doing everything we can
To protect the rights of the predators
Over their prey
We say it to them too many times
And then multiply that by two
Because, somehow, we think
We absolve ourselves of the guilt
Of arming predators
When we pray for the prey
Because we aren't pulling the trigger
So we convince ourselves
Prayers protect our prey
Even as we place the guns
In the hands of the predators yet again
So tell me when do we do more than pray
And take the action to actually protect the prey

Chatter Matter

Chatter, chatter, chatter
Sputtering words that don't matter
Spewing lies to the already enraged
To keep people encaged
Never stopped to see your role
Creating chaos takes its toll
As you drive wedges
By pushing people to edges
Spouting the latest hate
Fulfilling some misdirected fate
Your endless chatter
Makes you feel like you matter
Chatter, chatter, chatter

Disaster Around Me

The disaster around me
Looks too pretty to believe
How can this be a disaster?
My life today hasn't changed
Those policies that passed
I don't feel the effects… yet
So I look into the eyes
Of those who are feeling it
Try to understand that
My country isn't their country
Even though we are both citizens
What they live and what I live
Represents totally different realities
How do we change this?
I reach for your hand
Understand when you look at it askance
You have no reason to trust me
This disaster happening all around us
My complicity is implied
Though I will fight this disaster with my last breath
By your side, on the frontlines, in the background
Because I long for the day when we all join hands
And move forward through this disaster
Into a country you and I both claim
Into a country where you and I both stand proud
Into a country where you and I are equal
And no one can take that away from us

Rising Tide

I'll stand beside you
Hand in hand
Looking into the unknown
Waiting for the changes
We know are coming
Seeing nothing beyond
The rising tide
That threatens to sweep us away
Because we can't steer this monstrosity
We created when we sought to build life
On this cracked hull taking on a rising tide
Of hate coming our way
We thought we could show the world
How strong diversity makes us
As we each contribute to building this ship
Yet we failed to see all the cracks in the structure
The hate breaking us apart
As we dutifully repaired the splits
Vowing our love and compassion
Would be enough to bring us together
To float toward utopia
Where character is more important than bias
Where we lift each other instead of drowning
Those who are different
We hold hands and wade across the rising tide
Our only armor the love the world can't seem to find
I'll drown before I let go of love, so hold on tight
We're in this together

Never Was

What do I do?
All those things left behind
In the wake of loss
Not quite what they were
Not even what they could've been
You and me as lost as the next person
In the wake of a romanticized history
That imagines itself a utopia
That never existed
We talk about it with such reverence
Forgetting all the battle scars it left
Because to acknowledge those
Changes the story we want to believe
Into the reality of what really was
Or is it just the perspective changed
I wonder sometimes as I see your smile
Looking so much like it did and not quite the same
Your eyes still shine with excitement but also appear jaded
The confusion of experiences coalescing in the nostalgia
Wondering if forgiveness really did mean forgetting
Or maybe it just meant suppressing
Because everything we hide has a way
Of breaking through the barriers we create
To keep the past at bay
So we can remember the good
And forget the bad
So we can forgive the pain
So we can celebrate the fun
We look at each other with such
A carefully concocted façade
Knowing one brick will cause

The whole thing to crumble
And, yet, here we are
Accepting a history
That looks so perfect
And trying to get back to
What never was…

Battle Between Hope and Despair (a sonnet)

Temptation hides beneath all our shared words
Driving us toward a moment we can't control
Will the future be cut down by lost swords?
Words written in love on a hidden scroll

Our hearts searching for a healing embrace
Dependent on the promise of a new hope
Where the world judged change by a well-known face
Denied the chance to create a new trope

The past released to float adrift at sea
While the future seeks a new start
To grow a forest from a single tree
Left to sculpt truth from a broken heart

Nothing can grow in this abandoned pyre
Filled with destructive ice frozen in fire

Falling Apart

Your words fell apart
Before they reached my ears
I watched them formulate
Somewhere out there
Wanting so desperately to be heard
Crying for someone to understand
Reaching for someone to care
Knowing you could never be
What I needed
You spoke those words
And they floated by
In a jumbled mass of intention
Your fears butting up against my defenses
As you spoke one word and then the next
And watched those words fall at the wall
To my heart
Blocking us from finding common ground
Because to let you in meant abandoning
Some ancient belief I no longer even believed
Yet it stopped me from saying the words
A belief so strong I feared we'd both fall apart
If I spoke out loud
If I heard your words
So we stood speaking words that fell apart
Before they came close to their target
And the animosity grew
With each word that hit the defenses
Love couldn't even breach those walls
That stood between you and me
And the rest of the world
So the world crashed down around us

In a sea of words falling apart before they were even spoken
So where does this leave us
I want so desperately to lay down my arms
Open my arms
Embrace my fellow Earthlings
For us to find a path forward together
And yet we continue to speak so many words
Words and words and words
All falling apart
While we pretend to communicate
What happens when the words stop falling apart?
Do we fall apart?
Do we come together?
I'll keep trying if you will
Someday, someday, someday
I'm convinced we'll figure out how
To keep our words from falling apart

Change Adds Up

You dropped
A penny
A nickel
A dime
A quarter
In my hand
As you requested
We find a way to
Undo what had been done
To do what needed to be done
You told me each coin represented
A change that needed to be made
Small changes add up quickly
You promised me
As you walked away
Leaving me to change the world
One small coin at a time

Antiquated Beliefs

Incarcerated by your beliefs of whom I should be
Cuffs of expectation trapping me in an unwanted jail
Invisible bars silencing my words before I speak
Your image of me paints us both as villains in this game
Where a lack of evidence means as much as evidence
Judgment reigns down from mythology without discernment
To destroy any chance of creating lasting unity
Curses hidden in every promise of peaceful intent
You deceive yourself to cling to antiquated beliefs
Liberation only comes when you embrace factual proof

Artificial Distance

This distance between us
The one you insist exists
Is only in your imagination
You see a world where
We can never be more
Than enemies
Where our differences are more important
Than what we have in common
So you rant and rave
About how my existence diminishes yours
Though I can never see how
You live your life
I live mine
The two never intertwine
So how is it you think
My mere existence
Is enough to build walls between us
You don't see me
Even when I stand in front of you
You see what someone told you I was
Not who I am
Not a human being with thoughts and emotions
You see the declared enemy
Out to take what you can't admit you don't have
Trapped by your own need
To distance yourself
From the world in which you live
This world in which we both live
My contributions and yours
Both impact the community around us
We both inhabit the same Earth

Filled with resources to better both our lives
Yet you see a limited supply
You can't see how us both having enough
Makes life better for us all
You see only an enemy to keep at bay
Because yours fears, your hatred, your stereotypes
Shield you from the truth of life
Underneath the superficial
We both bleed, we both bruise, we both break
United we're stronger than divided
Imagine if we put down our shields of hate and fear
Got to know one another heart to heart
The distance we could bridge
Imagine the world we could create if we just
Saw each other's humanity

This Life I Lead

This life I lead
Down pathways in the dark
Where the light always seems fleeting
Disappearing into the shadows
Of memories haunting my steps
The click, click, click of my heels
On the asphalt taking me toward
The crunching gravel where
The clicks turn to
The crunch, crunch, crunch of my heels
Taking me toward the muddy trail
Where I discover
The sink, sink, sink of my heels
Slowing my progress
Reminding me where I came from
As I trudge along to find my way back
To the asphalt
And the determined
Click, click, click
Of heels finding the power to persevere
Until the moment I step into the comfort of home
And fling those shoes across the room
Embracing the soft
Pad, pad, pad of my bare feet
Across the floor
Feeling the embrace of home
Where all the need to be
This and that and the other
Dissolves in the woodwork
To remind me where love lives
To buoy me against the tides

Roiling outside my door
Where I forget to breathe
As I see the destruction wrought
By him and her and you and even me
As we struggle to travel the path
That brings us closer to compassion
Every day that we turn away from those in need
Another day lost that we could do something…
So I create my art to influence your heart
And hope that someday it will hit its mark
So that I can say this has all been worth it

This Matters, Right?

If this mattered
We would know
Wouldn't we
We pontificate
We grouse
We cry
We scream
We whisper
We lecture
We plead
See all this should matter
We know it should
So we vow
We'll take a stand
We promise
We'll speak up
It does matter
We insist
To anyone who will listen
Then we cry when
Our words go unheard
Nodding heads and amens
To words not truly heard
How many times
Must we insist
This matters
This matters
This matters
We know it matters
If only we understood
How to get the world to see

That what matters matters
Even when we disagree
It all matters
But will it still matter
When you and I can no longer
Remember
What mattered
Why it mattered
How it mattered
When it mattered
Or even
Who mattered…

Transpicuous Truth and Deception

Your words were anything but
Transpicuous
I listened to your cloudy thinking
Based on deceptive narratives
Wanted to correct you
Longed to speak to
The intelligence I know you possess
I know if you remove the blinders
Put on you by the manipulators
Who want you to never see
How their interests aren't yours
How their values aren't yours
How their gain isn't yours
You're far too smart
To keep falling for their obfuscation
Expand your knowledge base
Expand your sources
Expand your positions
Look for the transpicuous
In the muddled mess of obfuscation
Meant to keep you and I at odds
Maybe when you reach across the divide
And touch my fingers reaching back
We can find a way to bridge the confusion
With the truth
Letting the transpicuous deception
Fall to the rocks below
So the truth will finally be
Transpicuous to us both

Whispers in the Storm

I opened my mouth
Spoke the words you forbade
Whispered them quietly
In the midst of the storm
Hoping they'd fall on welcome ears
Somewhere in the distance
The truth of the moment
More important than
Bending to your will
I needed to be heard
No matter how difficult
It was to say the words
You only forbade them
Because speaking gave me power
You didn't want me to have
So when I looked you in the eye
Turned into the thunderstorm
Holding us in its thrall
Spoke the words to free me
You withered like a bloom
On a dehydrated plant
I watched you shrink
As my whisper reached a roar
In the midst of the storm
Where all the others
Who'd been forbidden to speak
Whispered into the storm
Spoke the truth you wanted hidden
Our whispered joining together
To create a roar that pushed
The storm back to the edge

So we whisperers could reach out
Take one another's hands
Step out of the clouds
Into the sunlight
Where our voices rang out
Like chimes in a gentle wind
Proclaiming our right to be there
We turned and
Whispered into the storm
One last time
As the storm consumed
You and your hate

Chaos

The winds of chaos
Blow through the peace we desire
Until we change us

Nothing Will Ever Be the Same

Nothing will ever be the same
Once you pull back those blinders
Allow your peripheral vision to see
The margins so easily ignored
When you look only in one direction
Seeing what fits your agenda
Never bothering to see
Those you hurt
Those who don't look like you
As you stare straight ahead
Into a world where everyone
In those margins you refuse to see
Seems somehow dangerous to you
As they go about lives
That looks mysteriously like yours
If you'd stop to see the person
Behind the stereotype
But, oh, no
That would require you to see
That what needs to change is
Your perspective
How do we change anything
When we refuse to change ourselves
But, oh, the day
You throw off those blinders
You'll never believe how free you feel…
And, what scares you the most
Is the thing you most need to embrace
Nothing will ever be the same…

Across the Wires

The wire electrified the connection
Between the distance we cultivated
Traveling along the wire
The words that would salvage
What we destroyed so easily
With thoughtless words
Sounding like a gong
On everything we once believed
Scrambling facts with utter disregard
Blending gossip into digestible smoothies
Lapped up as if it wasn't poison
Designed to kill everything we stood for
But the applause amplified the fiction
As it was sold as fact
And we forgot we are responsible
For the power we wield
For the power we shield
For the power we yield
Just so we could blame someone else
For the truth we don't want to face
That the power to send
All these messages across wires
Also comes with responsibility
To be accountable for
Fiction presented as fact
Fact distorted to look like fiction
But wires that connect make it so easy
To spread the rage
To spread the fear
To spread the fiction
That make us feel so enraged

We'd turn against our own families
Oh, the power of the wire
To expose those we thought we knew
For the haters they are
For the hysterics they are
For the hypocrites they are
So, know this, I see you
I see you for who you are
All because of what you sent
Across the wires

Seeing Symbols

Will this be the end?
Will you see what I see
Standing on the edge
As we scream at each other
Over symbols deemed sacred
By those wishing to control
Our every move
Symbols that could burn to ashes
With so little effort
Symbols future generations won't remember
Yet, we stand here valuing symbols over lives
Standing on opposite sides of this canyon
Screaming about how different we are
Refusing to see our similarities
Because if we unite
If we find common ground
If we value each other over symbols
We just might find enough power
To bring some order to chaos
Created by the divisiveness of hateful words
Reaching into our hearts to stoke the flames of fear
To keep us from seeing each other's humanity
Our frailty and our strength can unite us in love
If we can only stand here on the edge
Reach out across the divide
To see the world through each other's eyes
To see the symbols for what they are and how they're used
To see
        To see
                To see
                        Each other

Broken Reality

When reality is broken
Nothing less than wishful thinking takes over
We see a world where everything reflected back to us
Mirrors the broken reality in which we live
Where I can't see you and you can't see me
We see each other through the broken images
Created by the shards of a broken mirror
The truth distorted to feed the narrative
That keeps us from seeing beyond what we're told
Even when we know without a doubt
That the story we're told can't possibly be true
What we hate in another we're told is okay if it's our tribe
What we punish in another we reward if it's our tribe
What we love in another we hate if it's not our tribe
We look for the little clues to tell us what our tribe wants
Then scramble to reassemble the broken mirror
To reflect back to us what we want to see
Without ever admitting we've been manipulated
In the name of protecting our tribe
To keep us fighting each other so we're not paying attention
Because if the tribe is cohesive, there's always an enemy out there
If we can get the other tribe to turn on itself, it will self-destruct
Making our tribe feel all the more righteous and powerful
Even when the power belongs to neither tribe
But to those who broke the mirror...

Blood or Love

Today I read your words
Tears filled my eyes
I remembered a time
When I trusted you
Fully, completely, totally
We were family
I suppose we are still family
We share a bloodline after all
But I realized today
You won't have my back
Maybe you never did
I thought the blood we shared meant something
I truly did
As I watch you reveal the hate underneath
I realize how naïve I truly was
To believe that you accepted
The family I created because
Blood binds us
Because you could see
Love created my family
Because you could see
We are more alike than unlike
Through the family that truly supports me
So I guess
Maybe the family I created is more real than the one I was born into
Maybe blood really isn't such a strong bond, after all
Maybe love is a stronger bond than blood

Stretching for Common Ground

Can I stretch
Your words far enough
To reach make them
What I want to hear?
When you speak
Your words land
Like a thud on my heart
I wonder do you mean
What you say?
I always saw you
As compassionate and caring
Are you?
Have you been hardened so much
By life that you are no longer
The person I knew?
I look at your words
I see glimpses
Of the person I knew
Bleeding through the words
And I ask myself
What does this really mean?
Or maybe
I've changed so much
I can't stretch the past into the present
To meet you where we once were
So I reach out
I say the words I need to say
I hope you hear them
For what they are
I am sure
I know your heart

But maybe
That's just me
Stretching the truth
To find a place we can meet
Because I don't want
To believe the person I knew
Would embrace the lies
Of the haters…
I just can't believe it
So I'll continue to stretch
Until we can find
Stable, common ground
As we stretch toward one another

Tick, Tick, Tick

Sometimes I wonder
When all this will explode
I hear the tick, tick, tick
Like a clock counting down
The end flooding around our feet
Threatening to drown us
If this bomb we've built doesn't explode first
Destruction permeating our existence
Claiming we want peace
While we wage war
Our greed filling each moment
With more than our fair share
We pretend the tick, tick, tick
Has nothing to do with us
As we go about our selfish goals
We turn away from the destruction
Created by our carelessness
Our callousness ignoring all the damage
We don't want to be accountable for
Yet, on the tick, tick, tick goes
Our denial won't change the trajectory
Of the bombs we put in motion
Pretending they were fireworks
To celebrate a history we rewrite with ease
Pretending that a rewrite changes something
Even as the evidence rises around our feet
And time ticks, ticks, ticks
As we deny the reality in which we live
Covering our ears and closing our eyes
To shut out all the evidence

Ticking its way through our lives

Keep This Momentum

Keep this momentum
Rev it up but keep it steady
Sway to the rhythm
Snap to the beat
One step, two step
Forward, back, twirl
Eyes focused on mine
As we move toward this moment
Where we can both breathe
Our hearts connecting on the sly
Hiding beneath convention
Where truth rarely finds light
The electricity spreading through us
As we refuse to leave the floor
Embracing what we can never forget
Enlightened by memories of love
Heightened by determination to thrive
We stand on the precipice we abandoned
Time and again
Waiting for something to make this real
When all we can do is keep working
Toward the world we wish to inhabit
Where freedom doesn't come in shackles
Where boundaries don't reinforce hate
Where peace is more important than money
Where people matter more than power
Where equality is the norm not the exception
We grow weary in the work to unite
But this dance we dance must be danced
Time and again

If we're ever to make a difference

Bloody Words Exeleutherostomized

My tongue is bloody
And covered with toothmarks
From every word I've held back
When I should have spoken
I've watched atrocities from the safety
Of my couch
And shook my head but held my silence
I've heard the stories of the victims
And still held my silence
I've heard attacks on the vulnerable
And struggled to find a voice
I've survived traumas
And had my jaw snapped shut
When I tried to speak out
Silence stifled my voice
Even as I was accused
Yes, accused, not applauded
For even trying to speak up freely
To exeleutherostomize
To use my voice to make a difference
Accused of bluntness
Accused of aggressiveness
Accused of obnoxiousness
All for exeluerherostomizing
My experiences
Other's experiences
The facts of the pain
The injustices I witnessed
The injustices I heard
The injustices I experienced
Oh, yes, those accusations struck a blow

Into the depths of my soul
So I sank my teeth into my tongue
Until my mouth was filled with blood
I had to either spit it all out or choke on it
So I opened my mouth...

Burn the Facts

Build the fire
Until the flames
Lick the moon
Burning the truth
Pull out the facts
We thought frozen in reality
Throw them in the fire
Watch them burn up
Like they never existed
Turn to ashes
The truth unimportant
When it doesn't fit the narrative
So I leap into the fire
Burn my hands to retrieve
The facts you tried to burn
In the flames of the fantasy
You want life to be
But this is reality
The facts can't be burned
Just because you don't like them
The fire will only make the facts
Burn brighter in the face of your lies
So go ahead, build your fire
The facts won't be destroyed by the flames
Facts will rise up out of the ashes
To prove your deception
Today, tomorrow, forevermore

Live in Truth

Driven to believe
The lies uttered
So confidently
Because
Your lies were
So much easier
Than the truth
Living in denial
More comfortable than
Accepting the reality
Until I saw your lies
Destroy everything
In our path
Taking away possibility
Crashing into life
As I knew it
And still we stood
Drowning in those lies
Because you wanted
A world that never existed
Maybe I did, too
Yet those two worlds
Occupied completely different fantasies
You destroyed mine
As you fought for yours
Because in your mind
Accepting mine meant
Destroying yours
So better to destroy us both
Than to find a world where
We could live in truth

Voices Unheard

Pounding through my heart
Echoes of voices unheard
In the wake of undying pain
Division widening with each pulse
Driving our worlds apart
We lose our way
Fighting over beliefs
Ignoring solutions
Focused on distractions
Asking all the wrong questions
Ignoring all the right answers
Driven by separation
Pounding against the truth
As we refuse to see
What we've become
In the name of the unseen
To meet the expectations of the unknown
Until one day we look in the mirror
And see only the shattered shards
Of the division
Created by our inability to see
Ourselves in each other
While we fight each other
Those who benefit
Keep cashing in on the hatred
We swear we don't feel
Refusing to see that
We're stronger united than divided

Weakness Equals Strength

When you look at me
You see weakness
You can't see the strength
In compassion
You can't see the resilience
In understanding
You can't see the power
In honesty
You can't see the toughness
In love
No, when you see me
Offer the world
Compassion, understanding, honesty, love
You perceive my offerings as weakness
To be exploited
What you can't see is
The weakness
In the intolerance you spread
In the cruelty you support
In the greed you wield
In the hate you boast
I spend my life seeking unity
While you spend yours seeking divisiveness
So while you declare me weak
What I know is
Love spreads as it smolders
Hate however burns out fast
Love can survive the fire
While hate turns to ashes
So I'll run, walk, crawl
If necessary to keep

Uniting those seeking
Justice, connection, equality, peace
And someday, I know you'll see
Everything you thought made me weak
Was exactly where my strength emanated from
When you're left with only the ashes of your hate
To keep you warm as the blizzard buries you

Utopia

Days filled with
Sunny warmth with cool refreshing breezes
Sudden, short refreshing rainstorms
As we walk among
Roses, magnolias, blue spruce,
Fruit trees, vegetable plants with fresh, ripe sun kissed offerings
Modern, renaissance, art deco buildings
Rising up amidst the greenery honoring yesterday and today
As citizens from myriad backgrounds
Offer warm smiles, loving greetings, and make eye contact
As they dance through their days to a rhythm of joy
Stopping to appreciate all the animals who share life including
Dogs, cats, horses, cattle, frogs
Children dream of exploring the world to create betterment
Artists and poets inspire change as they share their work
Their efforts held in esteem to beautify and elevate
Because utopia seeks to manufacture, import, and export
Love, peace, and compassion to meet the needs of others
Graffiti becomes a celebrated artistic expression of
Love, peace, and compassion
Lovers aren't confined to norms but are left
Open to interpretation without judgment
Because the accepted conspiracy finds love solves more than hate
And style is left to the imagination where it can become individual expression
Where the memories of home evoke only a sense of belonging
Because no one is above another in a place where everyone matters
Everywhere you look you believe you've found the mythical Garden of Eden
Filled with fresh fruit and vegetables, and above all loving kindness
Because happiness continues to flourish even when challenges appear
So there's always the chance
I'll be home soon. We'll make love under the moon and laugh under the sun.
Watching Pegasus, unicorns, and the phoenix weave their magic

To create new beginnings while soaring above old pain opening new possibilities
Where everyone is excited about the stories of the microscope
Because every day brings
People of myriad backgrounds sharing meals
Life-affirming graffiti
Peaceful acceptance of one another
As utopia offers the crash of the beach on the shore on one border
And the voices welcoming visitors on the other borders
Because we refuse to allow hatred and fear to infect hearts and lead to violence
Making a lie of the postcard we send to the world promoting
Greenery and the ocean with a haiku promoting peace and love
Our utopia found us here where science and love met
And found a willing partner for change
In a world far too willing to leave behind
Those who don't conform
We welcome you to bring your love
But you must leave your hate at the border

I Want Someone to Love Me This Much

Remember as a child
Stretching your arms wide and saying
I love you this much and more
And marveling when larger arms than yours stretched out
And returned
I love you this much and more
As you laughed and leaped into
A warm, grandmotherly embrace
And thinking that much love had to be endless
As you wished for arms even larger
To express how much love you felt
Remember how free it felt to
Love this much and more
Have you ever felt that kind of love again?
Where has that kind of love gone?
Why can't we love one another that much now?
Why can't we look at our fellow earthlings and say
I love you this much and more
With arms stretched wide open
To embrace all those who need to be
Loved this much and more
Instead we draw lines in the sand
We pit ourselves against one another
We line up on sides and declare war
Over greed and territory and resources
Have you ever wondered what would happen
If we reached out to the whole world and said
I love you this much and more
Instead of constantly saying
I got mine, get yours
Or shut up, you don't deserve yours

Or you getting yours diminishes mine
Oh, what a utopia I dream of
Where we look at each other with love
Instead of distrust and hate and vitriol
A world where we stop pulling the ladder up behind us
A world where we readily look at each other as equals
A world where we work together for the betterment for all
Oh, yes, that's the utopia I dream of
The one where no one ever needs to say
I want someone to love me this much

Stay

Stay
The order rang through the air
I wanted to bark like a dog
Rffff
But instead I stopped in my tracks
Turned, stared, glared, waited
Met a hard gaze filled with hatred
A muzzle pointed right at my muzzle
I waited
Would you shoot
Would you bring me to heel
Would you simply imprison me
Your order rang through the air
My innocence no match for your hatred
You saw guilt before you saw humanity
You wanted nothing more than to lock me in a cage
Where you'd feel safe from my potential
All the while you demanded my loyalty
The same loyalty a dog would show you without hesitation
But which you'd never offer me
Such hatred ringing through that single word
Stay

Hands Up

Universal symbol of surrender
I give up
I give in
I surrender
All signaled with hands up
Don't shoot
Don't hit
Don't injure
All signaled with hands up
Standing before you
Hands up
What do you see
What impedes your vision
What prejudices guide your actions
Hands up
Begging you to see
The human being before you
Rather than your enemy
Can you even see surrender
For what it is?
Does it matter who I am
What crime deserves death
Without so much as a trial
Or even an arrest
There's a reason
We have a universal signal for surrender
Hands up
If I throw my hands up
Will you shoot me in the heart
Will you break my head
Will you usher in my demise

Do you see a threat in my
Hands thrown into the air
Or do you see surrender
For what it is
These are the unanswered questions
That strike fear in the hearts of
The guilty and the innocent alike
If I do everything right and end up dead
What good did it do to put my
Hands up

Take a Knee

Take a knee
A posture of protest
Wrapped in a gesture of submission
A peaceful message between violence
A tackle takes us to the ground
Reminding us the past builds the future
Heroes are often seen as troublemakers
In the moments they make us think
About those words we sing
About those words we salute
About the words we applaud
Tears in our eyes
Nostalgia rewriting history
So we can hold on to the glory
We think we exclusively possess
I kneel before no one
No, I kneel before no one
But today, oh, today,
In a moment of solidarity
For my brethren labeled
Sons of bitches for standing up
For what's right by
Taking a knee
I'll take a knee
While you chug your beer
While you stuff your face
While you fast forward through
The song you claim you love
One you've probably never
Really listened to
Oh, that troublesome third verse

Everyone likes to pretend doesn't exist
But there it is unforgettable
And demanding I pay attention
Remembering the apologetics
Proclaimed time and again
To convince my young mind
Singing about the glory of
Another's death was patriotic
Oh, but now as I think for myself
I just can't embrace those words
So I say to you
My friends
Blind loyalty will lead you astray
So tell me
Will you
Stand up for love
Or will you
Lie down with hate
Will you
Kneel down before power
Or will you
Take a knee for justice

Lost News

The news we should've heard
Lost in the drivel spewed
Telling us what to think
Before ever giving a single fact
Frame the story
Create the news
Direct the drive
Ignore the truth
In favor of a narrative
To push an agenda
To divide people
To create chaos
To wage war
So much lost
In the chatter
Of the non-news
Filling the airways
Losing the real news
In the margins of history
Driving the truth into the footnotes
Because who EVER reads the footnotes?
Who pays attention to the margins?
This narrative keeps us in an uproar
So we can't come together to change the future
This narrative kills any hope for unity and peace
This narrative loses the important
To keep the powerful in power
While keeping the weak on their knees
Someday, though, we have to find the news
Lost in the drivel drowning us all

Tape

I taped the words
To the page
Trapping them there for all time
Set against a background of dissent
Unwilling to budge from the truth
Reaching out to connect
Seeking greater understanding
To bring us together
So our strength will feed
One to another
Until we are a fortress
For those in need
We tape our movements
To life itself
In order to spread the idea
Our commonalities, our differences
Unite us, complement one another
Strengthen our intelligence, compassion, bonds
Drive us toward a greater future
Than we can accomplish apart
So tape those words
So tape those actions
Affix them to your life
Tape us together
So we can unite
For a future filled with
Love and hope
Taping together our rough edges

Rhythm & Blues

You and me
We were like rhythm & blues
I was rhythm
You were blues
Or maybe
You were rhythm
I was blues
I was never quite sure
As we tapped out a rhythm
As we sang the blues
Running in place
Never making it past
Our little square on the dance floor
Looking at those breaking free
To dance circles around us
Their rhythm not so bluesy
Tapped out in a hip-hop, sing song, rhyme
As we failed to see life changing around us
Stuck in thoughts of yesterday
Where our roles stepped on no toes
Just dancing the brain dead rhythm
Killing creativity in the process
Convincing ourselves we were special
Honoring tradition and feeling so elite
While all around us
Feet tapped out a new rhythm
Begging us to join
While we insisted what once was new
Hadn't grown old
Tap, tap, tap

Until one night
The blues broke us down
Forcing our feet to step outside the box
Tapping to a brand new rhythm
Freeing us from yesterday's nostalgia
As we wondered just who it was
Holding on to the rhythm
Holding on to the blues
We threw our heads back and laughed
Free to dance all the steps
The old and the new
The traditional and the progressive
Creating new steps to the old sounds
Applying old steps to the new sounds
Playing, playing, playing
Laughing, laughing, laughing
Feeling, feeling, feeling
Breaking all the rules
Someone else told us to follow

Just Out of Reach

There
Just out of reach
Is everything we desired
Where we thought we'd be
Standing side by side
Equal in this life
Seeing each other
For whom we are
Your hand reaching for mine
When I fall
My foot anchoring yours
When you reach higher
Standing together
To make a wall of love
That surrounds those
Who can't see
The good in you and me
We walk arms looped
In a rhythm we found
When we looked into each other's eyes
Where the sadness and the joy shone bright
Through the tears we shared
As we remembered those who came before
Fighting for the equality we still haven't found
Even though we're certain
It's right over there
Just out of reach…

That One Time

There was that one time
The time we stood in the crowd
Watching the world change before us
Just one of the masses
Seeing change before our eyes
Promising tomorrow would be better
Offering us change we could conjure
Between broken yesterdays and promised tomorrows
We stood there listening, believing, embracing
Knowing that we held the power in our hands
To bring the light to the dark night
To shine the sun through clouds
To illuminate the path to equality
Freedom standing in the shadows
Awaiting the power to change us all
Oh, yes, I remember that one time
That one time I believed we could
Change the world to be more inclusive
Oh, how I miss that one time
For years we'll be crying and longing for
That one time
When promise shined brighter than the sun

Recipe to Change the World

Gather the facts
Stir in some humanity
Add a dash of love
Sprinkle in some compassion
Mix in a good helping of honesty
Fold in a dollop of inspiration
Whisk in some empowerment
Top with some encouragement
Blend well
Bake until sparkly and bold
Share liberally with all one meets
Blending ingredients
With the diversity met
Along the way
Tweaking the recipe
Until it shines brighter
Than the hateful recipe
It encounters
From those wishing to
Destroy rather than create
Divide rather than unite
Deconstruct rather than construct
Nothing is tastier than a recipe
That brings the world together

In the Surf

I stepped my toe into the surf
Knowing if you did the same
We'd be connected by
The water between us
The tears of yesterday
Salting the sea
That finds its way
To the inlets and outlets
To the beginnings and ends
To the shores of every country
Ebbing and flowing
Taking the grains of sand
Squishing around my toes away
And bringing them back again
I thought of you and knew
It didn't matter
We can't see that
The ocean we share
Is part of the life
We don't share
Crashing toward you
Breaking toward me
Rushing between us
Seemingly calm and flat one minute
Angry and roiling the next
We bask in the sun
We shudder in the rain
Yet we forget
What touches you
Touches me
It all sounds so romantic

When you're thinking of
Someone you love
Connecting to you
On these little droplets
Passing between you
No matter the distance
But
Then there's the realization
It's not just you and me
But all the yous and mes
Inhabiting this planet
Connecting the dots
We don't want to connect
Because we're... we're... we're...
Not... you know
Friends
Someone told us we had to be
Enemies
Because we're... we're... we're...
Not... you know
The same
Even though we can both put a foot
In the surf and share a little bit of our selves
With everyone who has ever
Stood in the surf
Walked on a beach
Wiggled their toes in the sand
Sharing those bits of us
We leave behind wherever we are
So I stood there and thought about
You and me and him and her and...
All those who came before
All those who come now
All those who will come

And I wondered
If we all share so much
Why, oh, why
Do we insist on being
Enemies?

Haunting My Sunrises and Sunsets

Beautiful streaks of color
Across the sky
Oranges, reds, yellows
Glowing for all to see
Every sunrise and sunset
Over the waters
Over the mountains
Over the valleys
Over the deserts
Leave me standing here
Seeing what floats
Between sunrise and sunset
Seeing what hides
Between sunset and sunrise
All the days and nights
Embracing those secret longings
Of maybes and what ifs
Where the future could have been
What the present isn't
But can the future now be
What the past promised
Can we turn the fantasies
Haunting my sunrises and sunsets
Into a reality that fulfills the dream
Can I change your mind
Under cover of night?
Can I enlighten your heart
In the bright light of the sun?
Will you come with me on this journey
To a world where
Dystopia is a thing only for fiction

Not the future we face
If you take my hand and I take yours
Our differences finding a way to co-exist
Can we find a way to change all this
Before it's too late
As I watch another sunrise, another sunset
Come and go
Without a move away from hate toward love
I shiver knowing it's another day we let pass
Without embracing the best we could be
If we stood together instead of divided

The End of Democracy

Will we see
The end of democracy coming
The warning signs
Blowing through our lives
Like a cold winter breeze
Drifting the snow of democracy
Into drifts that drown us
In a sea of snowflakes
Dirty with the fighting
It takes to hold on to
The freedoms we
Believe to be protected
As we go about our lives
Ignoring as each one erodes
Trusting those we put in power
To put people over power
Forgetting the addictive power
Of power
Convince ourselves
We can change courses
At our next reset
The reset we believe is always there
But what happens when
The new beginning promised
Erases all signs of our choice
Will we fight for our representation
Or will we turn on one another
Allow tyranny to erase every clue
To the past we hold up as sacred
To the tradition we swear matters
To the myth of what we never were

Will we fight to become a
Better democracy or give in to become
Ruled by the fear that gives power
To greed and leaves us all
Wishing for a world
We imagine but can't quite create
Fighting isn't always bloody
But it always takes us to an ending
That births a new beginning
For better or worse…

Eternal Fight

This fight feels eternal
I watch you stand up
In ways I never could
I feel your heartache
Resonating deep in my core
As I shout into the wind
Hoping my words will reach you
"Don't stop
Don't ever stop"
Fighting for what's right
I'll stand side by side with you
I'll stand behind you
So you have a soft place to land
When they knock you down
I'll stand in front of you
To block the blow
I can't fight your battle
Because my experience isn't yours
But I can fight beside you
I can hear you
I can support you
I can be the one whispering in your ear
We won't ever stop
We stand together
We march together
We are the whispers
That become earwigs
We are the screams
That the wind can't drown out
We are the bodies
That wobble but don't stay down

We are the people
Who make up this movement
That can never stop
We are the change
We want to see
We are the truth
That refuses to lie
Perhaps this fight
Really will be eternal
But, we can't stop
We won't stop
Please don't stop
Even when
Especially when
They try to placate you
Even when there's no one left
To whisper in your ear
Don't stop
Maybe then you'll pass the torch
To new fighters
Offer them your support
And whisper softly in their ears
Don't stop
I've got your back
Because while we make progress
It just might be true
That this fight is eternal
Even when the battle feels won
Will it be?
Can we ever let our guard down?
All we can do is stand together
And hope that someday
Love and unity will win
Over hate and discord…

But, this fight just might be eternal
Even if it is
It's worth it
So, please, please, please
Don't stop
Don't ever stop

ACKNOWLEDGMENTS

Once again, thank you Loay for taking my abstract ideas for the cover and creating the cover. Thank you for the debates covering myriad issues that inspired some of the poetry in this book. Also, many thanks for always supporting me as I traverse this journey through both writing and life.

The photo, Women's March 2017 – Pennsylvania Ave, by Vlad Tchompalov was used with permission via Unsplash.

Thank you to my family, nuclear and extended, who had lively political debates that spanned the political spectrum when I was growing up. Their debates, disagreements, and discussions inspired me to keep searching for the facts hidden in the fiction and the fiction hidden in the facts to find common ground with those with whom I might not agree.

Thank you to Salem Poetry Project for listening to some of these poems and letting me see how they landed with an audience.

Thank you to my friends from myriad backgrounds who have helped me expand my knowledge and my understanding of the vast spectrum of life experiences around the country and the world.

All these conversations have influenced the poetry I write, and I thank you for that inspiration.

Thank you to all the friends and family who have read my work, encouraged me to keep writing, and inspired me along my journey.

OTHER BOOKS BY T. L. COOPER

Poetry:

Vulnerability in Silhouette

Strength in Silhouette

Memory in Silhouette

Reflections in Silhouette

Love in Silhouette

Short Stories:

Take a Chance & Other Stories of Starting Over

Soaring Betrayal

Fiction:

All She Ever Wanted

ABOUT THE AUTHOR

T. L. Cooper is an author and poet whose work aims to empower and inspire through an exploration of the human condition. Her poems, short stories, articles, and essays have appeared online, in books, and in magazines. Her published books include two collections of short stories, her *Silhouette Poetry books*, and a novel. She grew up on a farm in Tollesboro, Kentucky. When not writing, she enjoys yoga, golf, hiking, creating new plant-based recipes, and traveling. She currently lives in Albany, Oregon with her husband and three cats.

www.ingramcontent.com/pod-product-compliance
Lightning Source LLC
Chambersburg PA
CBHW051756040426
42446CB00007B/390